Linus Teaches Safety at School

Sandra J. Lofland-Brown
Luther L. Lofland, Jr.

ISBN 979-8-88540-604-8 (paperback)
ISBN 979-8-88540-605-5 (digital)

Christian Faith Publishing
832 Park Avenue
Meadville, PA 16335
www.christianfaithpublishing.com

Printed in the United States of America

Hello, kids, my name is Linus. Don't you think I am cute?

This is a real photo of me on the front of the book and this is a true story.

I am here today to talk to you about safety. I have learned about safety myself. One time, I fell down a flight of stairs and was badly hurt. I had to go to a dog rescue, which is kind of like foster care. Sometimes, children go to foster care for a while too.

I had to be in a doggie wheelchair like this one. Several people took me home from the rescue but brought me back because I became disabled. Then one day, a great man came and gave me a forever home. I call him Daddy. I love him, and he helps keep me safe.

My back has bumps on it and my legs do not work right. My legs do not work or look right because I was hurt. I look different from other dogs, although it is okay to look different. Every one of us is special even if we do not look like others. Children look different, but that is okay, too. My daddy's family members all have dogs. They do not look like me, but I like them anyway. I do not worry about feeling different. The dogs are all of different colors and sizes.

I can talk about many things, but today, I want to talk to you about being safe! You already know many facts about safety, and I want to remind you of the rules. Let us number our rules.

There are safety rules we should talk about. Let's review them.

1. Never play with matches, candles, lighters, and never play around a campfire.

2. Never take medicine that is NOT yours. Never drink anything you do not know what it is. Do not take candy from anyone you do NOT know. Have Halloween candy checked by an adult.

    Do you like my Halloween costume?

3. Learn the school's safety rules about tornadoes, fire, and disaster rules.

4.   It is very important to learn your home address. If you would get lost, stand still, so when someone you trust comes to find you, tell them your name. Then tell them where you live and who you live with.

5.   Learn to call 911 so you can help a person if they are hurt.

6.   Never jump into any pool or lake until you have permission from an adult.

7.   Never chase a ball or anything out in the street because a car or truck could hit you!

8.   Never put a plastic bag over your head or anyone else's head as you cannot breathe.

9.   Tell mom and dad not to put your name on your bookbag or clothing because people will know your name and could ask you to come with them as you would think they know you.

8

10. Be very careful if someone wants you to get in a car with them or like a big van without windows. I am sorry to say that some people are not nice and play tricks on kids like you, and they are bad tricks.

11. Have a "code word" with your parents. Learn that word and do NOT go with anyone who does not know the code word.

12. You will learn about Internet safety as you get older. Report any bullying, bad pictures, or someone wanting to meet you somewhere. Never share your address, phone number, or any personal information.

13. There are lots of safety rules about the Internet you must follow.

14. If you see a gun, do not touch it and run for help! Tell someone older right away as guns can kill people.

15. Do not go into anyone's house without asking an adult's permission. Some people trick kids by telling them they have baby kitties or puppies to get them to come into a car, van, or house.

I have another kind of safety rule to talk about, called Personal Safety. Personal means about your body. I want to keep my body safe, and I know you do, too. Your body belongs to you. I do not even like to tell you this, but sometimes, people try to play tricks on you and touch the private parts of your body. What are the private parts of your body? They are the parts covered by your underwear or a bathing suit.

Let's talk about good touches. I like to see kids give "high fives" or a pat on the back. I like a nice pat on my head or back as a good touch.

I do not like bad touches like when someone hits, smacks, or touches my private parts of my body. My body belongs to me, as I have told you before!

These parts are private areas. You don't want others to see or even touch your private parts; they belong to only you. A doctor might have to check your body sometimes, but that is one reason someone should touch your private parts, or maybe when someone is bathing you, to help you keep clean. I love a nice bath. Look at me all wrapped up in my towel.

Sometimes people try to play tricks on you and touch the private parts of your body. That is when you yell NO and run and TELL someone right away and keep telling until someone believes you! It is important to make the bad touching stop. The most important rule is that touching was NOT your fault! Someone was playing a bad trick on you. It is important to remember, so let me say again that bad touches are NOT your fault!

My grandma used to teach personal safety or body safety at schools, and I have heard her sing a wonderful song that she wrote. It is called "Yell and Tell." She had puppets named Archie and Abbie, which taught children safety rules and songs.

Let me read or sing this song to you. Maybe your teachers can give you a copy of the song and sing it with you sometimes. Sometimes, a song can stay in your head and help you remember safety rules from "Yell and Tell."

Wow, I have had fun telling you about myself and my safety rules today. I hope you will want to listen or read my book over and over again. You might want to sing my song "Yell and Tell."

Bye!

Woof!

Hey, how did those cats get in my book? This is a dog book!

Linus's Closing Thoughts

The children of our world are our most precious assets! We must take each child's life seriously and help them grow and develop into productive and wonderful humans. How can we do this?

This book, *Linus Teaches Safety at School*, will help us all to help make the children into loving, caring, and safe adults.

Over four hundred thousand children and youth are placed in foster care in the United States each year www.acf.hhs.gov/cb. There are also untold numbers of children who do not know basic safety rules of how to survive in today's hectic, cruel, and sometimes traumatic world. There are unfortunate children who suffer from disabilities and handicaps, and they think they are different from others; because of this, many will meet failure in life.

This book is about Linus, a real dog, a true story, who suffered through unsurmountable obstacles in his short years of life, but he found love and compassion to overcome these obstacles because a man believed in him.

Linus was a shelter dog several times with disabilities and handicapped in a wheelchair, but he is safe and happy today. We want every child to be safe and happy today!

Let's all learn to teach children from their early years about the important things in life and how valuable they all are. As a matter of fact, let's treat our pets in the very same way. Adopt shelter dogs and cats whenever possible and show them the love and respect they deserve. Thousands of pets are waiting for someone to love them and adopt them

About the Authors

Sandra Lofland-Brown is a retired social worker majoring in the field of child abuse prevention. She graduated from Saint Mary of The Woods College in Terre Haute, Indiana, and the Committee for Children out of Seattle, Washington. Sandra wrote her own scripts for teaching elementary students personal safety with puppets, Archie and Abby, which she made, and music, by the use of her original song "Yell and Tell."

Sandra has received the "Award of Merit" for her noteworthy contribution to furthering the profession of play therapy, from the Indiana Associates of play therapy. She also received the Cherish the Children Award from Prevent Child Abuse of Indiana.

Sandra has four children, seven grandchildren, and three great-grandchildren. She is married to Kenneth Brown.

Luther Lofland shares his wealth of knowledge from his forty-plus years of experience working with special needs students and adults. Lofland earned a master's of education from Indiana State University in the areas of learning disabilities and emotionally handicapped licensures. His experience spans working with individuals in schools and mental health inpatient and outpatient settings. He taught for over seven years as a special education teacher in an inpatient rehabilitation hospital. After teaching in public schools for thirty-four years, Lofland said, "My experience has been heart-wrenching and rewarding at the same time. I have worked with families and students, observing students and families, teaching new strategies and social skills that will benefit them forever."

Lofland went on to say that he has always been an advocate for the underdog who struggles with success, including Linus, the dog he rescued, who had been physically and emotionally abused by six other owners before finding him forever home.

Lightning Source UK Ltd.
Milton Keynes UK
UKHW050922181222
414024UK00005B/78